The A-8 of Learning

Chris Duncan-Scott

Copyright © 2024 Chris Duncan-Scott

All rights reserved.

ISBN: 9798880135967

DEDICATION

This book is dedicated to my Mum.
Sadly, she'll never get to read it but it's her spirit for getting on with things that allowed me to find the courage to write my first book and achieve a dream.

I'm also dedicating this to David.
My husband, my constant support, and my business partner.
He's a very important half of the Acceler8 story.

And a word for Bo. Our dog. If you're a dog person, you'll get it.

Mum, David, Bo – this is for you.

CONTENTS

	Acknowledgments	i
1	A is for…	Pg 1
2	B is for…	Pg 8
3	C is for…	Pg 14
4	D is for…	Pg 18
5	E is for…	Pg 23
6	F is for…	Pg 27
7	G is for…	Pg 32
8	H is for…	Pg 37
9	I is for…	Pg 41
10	J is for…	Pg 45
11	K is for…	Pg 48
12	L is for…	Pg 51
13	M is for…	Pg 55
14	N is for…	Pg 59
15	O is for…	Pg 63
16	P is for…	Pg 67
17	Q is for…	Pg 71

The A-8 of Learning

18	R is for…	Pg 74
19	S is for…	Pg 77
20	T is for…	Pg 81
21	U is for…	Pg 85
22	V is for…	Pg 88
23	W is for…	Pg 92
24	X is for…	Pg 96
25	Y is for…	Pg 101
26	Z is for…	Pg 105
27	And now 1-8…	Pg 109

ACKNOWLEDGMENTS

There are many people to acknowledge in the journey to getting this book into print and onto your e-readers.

Some are name checked through the course of the book, others need listing here. So, let's acknowledge the following:

Carole English, for inspiring me to want to work in learning and development in the first place.

David Morley for being so kind with our original brand identity and those early exhibitions. I can't say a big enough thank you.

Team Acceler8 for being part of what we're building together. This has never been a one person show – collectively, we are brilliant.

Finally, to all the talented learning experts and facilitators I've had the joy of working with over the years, so many to name that it would take another book, but I hope you know who you are!

This book has only been possible because of everything I have learned from others.

#BeHappyBeHuman

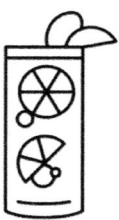

A IS FOR ACCELER8

In an 'A-8' it seems only fair that the first chapter is dedicated to why I'm writing the book. The Acceler8 story really does sum up the journey we've been on, as well as the approach that my co-founder (and husband) David and I take to our business.

Our story started back in 2015. I was working in London and David was flying all over the place in aviation. We had family and friends staying and I had my usual commute home one September evening. I'd arrived home at about 8pm and everyone was already on after dinner drinks.

I was playing catchup.

A few gins and tonics later and I'd been talking about my day. It had been a particularly rough period in that job for me and I knew that the daily commute just wasn't for me. You could see the people who thrived with that life… but it wasn't me. The normal dinner conversation turned to those immortal words from our friend Stanley Tau. He simply asked what was stopping us from doing it for ourselves.

It might have been the gin, it might have been the universe, it might just have been spontaneous, but we said yes. Even better, we'd do it right now. We logged into Companies House to register the company – we'd sort the detail out another time.

We needed a name. We agreed we needed something that stood out. I thought replacing a series of letters with a number was 'cool' (no judgement needed here!). We picked a few names, searched them… they'd already been used. We kept searching and eventually found that Acceler8 Training was available. By default, the company was born.

With hindsight – no wonder it was free, nobody wanted training in their company name. It was outdated, but we needed a company name, and we needed it right away. So that's what we registered. I shut the laptop, we celebrated with more gin and eventually went to bed – so I could get up at 5am to do the commute all over again.

The following morning, I caught the normal train to London Victoria and had my normal daily text conversation with David. Last night had been fun, we didn't really mean it, we would just carry on as we are and let someone else set up a learning consultancy – we didn't really know the first thing about running a business so it would be much safer that way.

Next up, my normal check of my personal email.

An email from Companies House was top of the list. I opened it and saw confirmation of our company name… along with a full list of our newly acquired Director responsibilities. My heart was in my mouth. There was no going back.

After a few days of nervous laughter and 'could it really work' conversations, I went into work and had a long conversation with my boss. I shared why I wanted to set up on my own – meaning I could be there more easily for my Mum and Dad if they needed me and how my current role would make that difficult.

Pauline listened, she asked some questions, she listened some more and then we had a lovely conversation about why I thought it was the best thing. She helped me secure some freelance work with the company I was leaving, which helped us through our first year. There are people who stand out in your career and Pauline is very much one of those.

There was a lot we didn't know. We didn't know how difficult it would be to attract clients, to budget, to forecast, to get paid on time, to cope with uncertainty… owning and leading a business equips you with a robust skillset – and a few more grey hairs and wrinkles.

The first year was good. Year two, the work dried up – to this day I still have no idea why that happened. I'd only ever done good work for the company I was freelancing for and suddenly… nothing.

Ghosted.

I'd love to understand why… although I have come to terms with that now. It says more about them than me. It's something you need to get used to if you work in the freelance or self-employed world – not everyone can cope with it. There have been times when I've not coped with it awfully well.

We worked hard, we looked at how we could take the business forward and make enough money to live comfortably.

Another random conversation one day with another friend, David Morley, and suddenly we were signing up to do our first ever trade show. We went big – straight to the NEC. David designed us a beautiful stand and a shiny new identity to replace the one I'd done in about 3 minutes on the internet… and Acceler8 as you know it today was born.

I remember being in Costa Rica with clients and bouncing around when I saw the new company look and feel. It was bright, warm, trusted… and the word training had been reduced to nearly nothing. The focus was entirely on Acceler8 with the infinity symbol (also the number 8 on its side… there's still a nod to the number 8 on its side in our current identity).

Who knew there was a pandemic coming? We certainly didn't. Had we known that was going to arrive just as we were in full stride, we might have done things differently. That threw us off track for a few years. It took everything we had to keep the business alive. It took a fair amount of what we didn't have too. We made the right moral decisions. We didn't lose anyone during actual Covid, we kept pay at 100%, we did everything we could to make the Covid experience as good as it could be for our colleagues.

We also missed some mortgage payments and a few credit card payments to make sure we could do that. We lost a lot personally during that time, but David and I still stand by the decisions we made – putting our colleagues first all the way through.

Why am I sharing this? Well, I know it's a dream for so many to do what we've done, so it's best to go into it with your eyes open. Take all the advice you need but find your own path. Don't try and copy someone else. If anyone is kind enough to give you time or advice, don't repay them by trying to copy exactly what they do – that happens more than you might think… and yes, if you've done it, I've probably made a mental note…

As I write this book, we are in a fantastic position as a business. We have more clients than we've ever had, we've grown every year since we started trading, we've developed learning that we're very proud of, we've got clients that are our biggest fans and we've got the very best people in the business on our team.

We've still got big ambitions. We want to be the most sustainable learning consultancy in the world. We want to live up to our new Global name – we're becoming a global brand that operates locally, doing good business in a good way. We want to keep on growing and nurturing our talent, and doing the very best we can for our clients.

We work across so many sectors, topics, and audiences. We've designed learning that has been delivered to tens of thousands of people across the world. We've looked at our client list and we're confident that in some way, we impact most people's daily life because of the people we work with.

So... back to this book writing malarkey! In the spirit of getting to the point quickly (a chapter all on its own), I've given a summary of each letter and some food for thought. I hope it's an opportunity to reflect, to think about what you believe and to be open to both similar and opposing points of view – that's the point of learning after all.

This is my A-8 of learning – a whistlestop tour of stuff I've learnt, things I value and elements that can make learning better. It's not an exhaustive list – I would need to write hundreds of books to cover everything.

Ready? Let's go!

B IS FOR BIAS IN LEARNING

Buckle up (another B), because we're about to embark on a journey into the world of biases in learning – a journey as intricate and surprising as finding your way through Hampton Court Maze.

Now, before you start fretting that this is about pointing fingers and declaring, "Aha! Bias!", let's set the record straight: this is about understanding, not accusing. It's about introspection, not interrogation.

There are well documented arguments that making a big deal of biases creates bias where there is none.

I think there is real value in the concept of bias – being open to why we make the judgements we do can help us approach human situations entirely differently.

Spotting the Chameleon: Recognising Bias

Recognising bias is like trying to spot a well-camouflaged chameleon on a particularly vibrant bush. It's there, alright, but it blends in seamlessly. Bias can hide in our assumptions, our language, and even in who we decide should answer the challenging questions in a learning environment.

The Everyday Bias

Consider this: have you ever found yourself surprised when someone doesn't fit your mental mould? Maybe it's the IT whizz who's also a conga champion or the soft-spoken individual who turns out to be a powerhouse in a debate. These moments of surprise are tiny windows into our biases – those preconceived notions we have about how people should be and act. We all have them.

Bias in Learning Materials

Take a good, hard look at the learning materials you use or

create. Are they a one-size-fits-all, or do they consider diverse perspectives? Often, learning materials are unintentionally skewed, presenting a narrow view of the world. It's like having a history book that only talks about the victors, leaving out the other side of the story. It would be easy for us to get carried away with a particular learning method, but we'd run the risk of alienating some of our participants – and that just wouldn't work.

The Bias of the Facilitator

Even the most experienced facilitators can inadvertently let bias colour their thoughts and judgement . It might manifest in favouring certain learners, assuming some will find the material easy (or difficult), or even in the examples they choose to use. This bias isn't malice; it's just an uninvited guest that's crept into the party – and one we should impolitely ask to leave. It's not easy – I catch myself playing that game all the time.

The Bias Blind Spot

We've all got a bias blind spot – that area where we fail to recognise our own biases. It's like trying to tickle yourself; it doesn't work because you can't surprise your own brain. In the same way, it's hard to see our biases because they're our 'normal.' It's just how we see the world around us.

Tackling the Beast: Addressing Bias

That title is the equivalent of click bait in the book. Try not to think of bias as a beast. It's a big animal, but little steps towards taming it are going to be more effective than a violent assault.

So how can we all start to take those small steps to addressing our biases?

1. **Self-Reflection**: It starts with you. Reflect on your biases. It's about as comfortable as sitting on a whoopee cushion in a quiet room, but it's necessary.
2. **Seek Feedback**: Sometimes, you need an outside perspective. Ask colleagues or students to point out when they think bias is creeping into your material or teaching.
3. **Embrace Diversity**: Ensure your learning materials and examples represent a broad spectrum of perspectives. It's like making a playlist that includes more than just your favourite two artists. (Bucks Fizz and ABBA if you're interested...)
4. **Inclusive Language**: Words matter. They can build bridges or walls. Use language that's as inclusive as a big family hug at a reunion.
5. **Diverse Learning Methods**: People learn differently. Mix up your teaching methods to cater to a range of learning styles, from visual learners

to those who prefer hands-on experiences, to those who learn more from reflection and curious questioning.

The Ripple Effect of Bias in Learning

Consider the impact of bias on learners. It can shape their self-image, their participation in the learning process, and even their future aspirations. It's a bit like planting seeds – the environment you create can determine whether those seeds flourish or wither.

Bias in learning isn't just a 'classroom' issue. It extends to the workplace, to workshops, and even to informal learning environments. It's about creating spaces where everyone feels they have an equal opportunity to learn and grow.

Here's some questions we can ask ourselves…

1. When was the last time I actively sought to identify and challenge my biases?
2. How can I ensure a range of voices and perspectives in my learning environment?
3. In what ways might my biases be affecting my expectations of others' abilities and contributions?
4. How can I create more inclusive and diverse learning experiences that cater to a variety of learners?

5. What steps can I take to continually educate myself on the biases that exist in learning environments?

For me, addressing bias in learning isn't about embarking on a witch hunt for every possible prejudice. It's about acknowledging that biases exist, understanding their impact, and taking steps to create a more inclusive, equitable learning environment.

So, arm yourself with awareness, empathy, and a commitment to continuous improvement. Let's make our learning spaces as welcoming and as enriching as they can be – and watch engagement soar.

C IS FOR COLLABORATION

Imagine you're trying to assemble a puzzle, but you're not the only one holding the pieces. Everyone around you has a few puzzle pieces in their hands, and no one can complete the picture alone. This is what learning in any environment looks like.

It's not a solo act; it's a team sport.

The Myth of the Lone Learner

There's this old myth that learning is a one-person show. You sit down, you read the books, and you absorb knowledge. Simple, right? Wrong. I don't think that's how it works, especially when we're talking about crafting a learning strategy. Learning is social, dynamic, and interactive.

The Power of Listening

You've got ideas. So does everyone else. If you don't listen, you miss out. Stakeholders - be they learners, colleagues, managers, or even external clients - have valuable insights that can shape a more effective learning experience. Listening isn't just about being polite; it's about being smart.

The Ripple Effect of Learning

Imagine you drop a new learning strategy like a stone in a pond. The ripples are the impact. That stone affects more than just the water it touches first—it sends waves out far and wide. That's what your learning strategy does. It impacts every stakeholder in ways you might not immediately see. The impact will be there whether your strategy is good or bad.

Building Bridges, Not Walls

Learning strategies should build bridges between people, departments, and goals. This isn't just feel-good talk—it's a solid strategy. When you build bridges, you share insights, resources, and support.

A Simple 'Building Relationships' Model

Let's keep it straightforward with a model you can remember: the 3Cs of Collaboration. My apologies, I've used this for years, but I don't know who attribute it to.

1. Communication: Clear, consistent, open. Talk and, more importantly, listen.
2. Commitment: Everyone should feel they're part of the journey, committed to the same end goal.
3. Compromise: Be ready to bend. Not every idea will fly, and that's okay.

Bringing Stakeholders on Board

Want to ensure your learning strategy sticks? Get your stakeholders involved early and often. When they contribute, they're invested. And when they're invested, they want to see things succeed as much as you do.

Practical Steps to Improve Stakeholder Relationships

1. Regular Check-Ins: Don't wait for the annual review. Have regular coffee chats, share updates, ask for feedback.
2. Shared Goals: Define what success looks like, together. Make sure everyone's eyeing the same prize.
3. Celebrate Wins: Big or small, when there's a win, make sure everyone knows and feels part of it.
4. Acknowledge Expertise: Everyone's an expert at something. Recognise their strengths and leverage them.
5. Recognise that knowledge ownership will often sit with someone else. Learning experts own the engagement with that knowledge – often a relationship dynamic that is forgotten.

In a nutshell

Learning isn't a one-person job. It's a symphony of voices, ideas, and efforts. The more we listen to and work with our stakeholders, the more harmonious and effective our learning strategies become.

Remember, no one has all the pieces, but together, we can complete the puzzle beautifully. So let's step out of the silo and into the circle. Let's collaborate, let's listen, and let's learn. Together.

D IS FOR DIGITAL LEARNING

In a world where digital is often seen as impersonal or distant, let's flip the script and explore how digital learning can be a vibrant, engaging, and human-centric avenue for learning. Far from being the cold, unfeeling cousin of traditional classroom learning, digital learning, when done right, can be a lively and effective method of knowledge acquisition.

Let's dive into the different types of digital learning and unpack their pros and cons, keeping 'happy humans' at the heart of it all.

1. eLearning Courses

These are structured courses offered online, often self-paced and consisting of text, video, and interactive activities.

Advantages:

- Accessibility: Learners can access these courses anytime, anywhere.
- Self-Paced: Individuals can learn at their own speed, revisiting content as needed.

Disadvantages:

- Lack of Personal Interaction: It can feel isolating without the presence of an instructor or peers.
- Requires Self-Discipline: Some learners may struggle with the self-directed aspect.
- The temptation to click at speed and hope for the best if there is an assessment.

2. Webinars

Live online sessions where a facilitator leads a presentation, often with the opportunity for participant interaction.

Advantages:

- Real-Time Learning: Immediate interaction with facilitators for questions and clarifications.
- Wide Reach: Allows participants from different locations to join.

Disadvantages:

- Limited Interactivity: Large webinars may not offer much individual interaction.
- Technical Issues: Reliant on good internet connections and technology.

3. Virtual Classrooms

An online environment simulating a traditional classroom, where facilitators and participants interact in real-time.

Advantages:

- Interactive: More opportunities for discussions and group work.
- Structured Learning Environment: Mimics the traditional classroom setup.

Disadvantages:

- Less Flexibility: Usually requires participants to be online at set times.
- Technology Dependency: Requires stable internet and compatible devices.

4. Gamified Learning

Incorporating game elements (like point scoring, competition, rules of play) into the learning process.

Advantages:

- Highly Engaging: Games can increase motivation and interest.

- Interactive and Fun: Makes learning more enjoyable and memorable.

Disadvantages:

- May Overshadow Content: The fun aspect can sometimes overshadow the learning objectives.
- Not Suitable for All Topics: Some subjects may not lend themselves well to gamification.

5. Microlearning

Delivering content in small, specific bursts, often focused on a single learning outcome.

Advantages:

- Efficient: Quick and to-the-point learning.
- Easy to Digest: Breaks down complex topics into manageable chunks.

Disadvantages:

- Surface-Level Learning: May not be suitable for deeply complex topics.
- Fragmented Experience: Can feel disjointed if not well integrated.

Digital Learning with 'Happy Humans' in Mind

The key to successful digital learning is to keep it human-centric. It's about designing these experiences to be engaging, interactive, and emotionally resonant. This means:

- Prioritising user experience in design.
- Ensuring content is relevant and relatable.
- Incorporating social elements where possible, such as forums or group projects.
- Providing support and feedback channels.

In a nutshell

Digital learning, when done thoughtfully, can be a highly effective way to learn. It's not about replacing the human element; it's about enhancing it with the power of technology. As we embrace the digital age, let's do so with the aim of creating learning experiences that are not just efficient and effective, but also joyful and human. Remember, at the heart of every screen and every click, there should always be a 'happy human' learning and growing.

P.S.
The irony of writing this chapter is not lost on me. It took a pandemic for me to embrace and champion digital learning – and that was driven by survival as a business. Where I think it worked for us, was taking everything we knew about engagement and applying it to digital. I'm absolutely against a 'click, click, click, assess' mentality – I'm more in favour of holding attention all the way through.

E IS FOR EXPERIENTIAL LEARNING

Imagine if we learned to swim by sitting in a classroom, discussing the theory of buoyancy, and never actually getting wet. Sounds ridiculous, doesn't it? This is where experiential learning comes in – it's the plunge into the pool of learning, rather than just dipping your toes in. And no, we're not talking about trust falls in the office (thank goodness) or constructing rafts out of office supplies.

It's about learning by doing, which often reaps far greater rewards than traditional learning methods.

What is Experiential Learning?

Experiential learning is the process of learning through experience and is more specifically defined as "learning through reflection on doing." It's hands-on, immersive, and often involves a real-world or simulated application of skills and knowledge. Think of it like learning to cook by cooking, not just reading a recipe book.

Why Dive In?

1. Retention: When you actively engage in doing something, you're more likely to remember it. It's the difference between reading about how to ride a bike and wobbling around on two wheels until you get the hang of it.
2. Relevance: Experiential learning ties learning to real-life situations. This makes the learning feel more relevant, and, let's be honest, less like a chore.
3. Engagement: It's generally more engaging to participate in an activity than to passively listen to a 'trainer'. More engagement means a better learning experience.
4. Develops Critical Skills: It helps develop essential skills like problem-solving, critical thinking, and adaptability – skills that are crucial in today's ever-changing workplace.

Examples of Experiential Learning in Organisations

1. Simulations: These are a bit like video games, but for learning. Imagine a simulation for project management where learners navigate through a

project from start to finish, making decisions and dealing with issues along the way.
2. Role-Playing: Not the behind closed doors at home kind but role-playing different workplace scenarios. This could be handling a difficult customer or negotiating a contract. That's the theory – but in practice so many people hate role-play, that's why we've got a whole chapter on it later in the book. Nevertheless, it is an example...
3. Shadowing: Nothing beats the experience of being in the actual environment where the skills will be applied.
4. Hands-On Workshops: This could be anything from a leadership bootcamp to a first-aid training session where you practice bandaging someone.
5. Team Projects: Collaborating on a project can be a great learning experience, especially when the project has real-world implications.

In a nutshell

Experiential learning isn't about replacing traditional learning methods; it's about complementing them. It adds the depth and flavour to learning that can sometimes be missing in more conventional approaches. It's the difference between reading about Paris and strolling along the Seine.

So, next time you're planning a learning activity, ask yourself: how can I make this experiential? How can I take this from theory into practice? Remember, sometimes the best way to learn something is just to dive in and do it. And who knows, it might just be more fun than those dreaded trust falls.

F IS FOR FACILITATION

I love an analogy, so picture yourself at the helm of a learning session. You're not just imparting wisdom; you're steering a ship of diverse learners through the seas of knowledge and discovery. To be the captain they deserve, you need a set of key skills in your facilitator's toolkit.

Let's explore these essential skills: Listening, Questioning, Objectivity, Summarising, Intervention, Empathy, and Engagement, and discover how you can master each one.

1. Listening

Good facilitators listen more than they speak. It's not just about hearing words; it's about understanding the message behind them. In a learning environment, this means being fully present. When a participant speaks, give them your undivided attention. Avoid the temptation to think about your response while they're still talking.

Tip: Practice active listening. This involves nodding, making eye contact, and occasionally paraphrasing what the speaker has said to confirm understanding. It needs to be practiced, otherwise it will be fake.

2. Questioning

Asking the right questions can be the difference between a light bulb moment and a flickering candle. Good questions stimulate thinking, encourage exploration, and can guide learners to discover insights themselves.

Example: Instead of asking yes/no questions like "Do you understand?", ask open-ended questions such as "What are your thoughts on this approach?"

3. Objectivity

Facilitators must be the neutral party in the room, especially during discussions or when conflicts arise. This means setting aside personal opinions and biases and focusing on what's best for the learning process.

Hint: If you have a strong view on a topic, acknowledge it and then step back. Say something like, "I have my own thoughts on this, but I'm more interested in hearing yours."

4. Summarising

Summarising is an art. It involves distilling the key points from a discussion or section of learning into a concise and clear format that everyone can understand.

Example: At the end of a session, say, "Let's recap the main points we've covered," and then list them succinctly.

5. Intervention

There will be moments when you need to steer the conversation back on track, handle disruptive behaviour, or provide additional support. Intervention should be done tactfully and assertively.

Tip: Use phrases like, "Let's refocus on the main topic," or, "I appreciate your enthusiasm, I'm interested to hear what others think too."

6. Empathy

Understanding and relating to the feelings of your learners is crucial. Empathy helps in creating a safe and supportive learning environment.

Example: If a participant seems frustrated or confused, acknowledge their feelings with a comment like, "I understand this is challenging; how can I assist you further?"

7. Engagement

Finally, engagement. The goal is to keep learners interested and involved. This requires a mix of energy, enthusiasm, and the ability to make learning relevant and enjoyable.

Hint: Use interactive elements like group activities, real-life scenarios, and questions that prompt participants to think and respond.

In a nutshell

Facilitation is not just about knowledge delivery; it's an art form that requires a blend of skills. By mastering listening, questioning, maintaining objectivity, summarising effectively, intervening when necessary, showing empathy, and engaging your learners, you're not just a facilitator; you're a guide, a mentor, and a catalyst for learning.

So, as you step into your next facilitation role, ask yourself: How can I apply these skills to create a more effective and enriching learning experience? Remember, the best facilitators are not those who speak the most, but those who bring out the best in their learners.

I think there's probably another book in here somewhere! When I look at our signature Train The Facilitator experience it covers so much more than I have space for here.

As a facilitator, you are always learning new ways to handle situations and let the participants guide the session. None of us will ever stop refining our facilitation capability – there's always something new to discover or learn.

G IS FOR GAMIFICATION

Back to my analogies...

In the ascent to the summit of effective learning, gamification is a path lined with engagement, motivation, and a bit of healthy competition. But what exactly is gamification in the context of learning, and how does it transcend being just a game with a learning tag slapped onto it?

Let's explore the world of gamification, its power to transform learning experiences, and the fine line between an effective learning tool and an overplayed game.

Gamification in learning involves applying elements of game playing, such as point scoring, competition, and rules of play, to educational activities. It's not about turning learning into a game per se; rather, it's about using game mechanics to enhance the learning experience, making it more engaging and memorable. In short, it can increase knowledge transfer significantly.

Using the Power of Play to Unleash Learning

1. Engagement: Gamification introduces an element of fun that can help capture and maintain learners' attention.
2. Motivation: Through points, badges, rewards, and leader boards, learners are motivated to participate and progress.
3. Immediate Feedback: Games often provide instant feedback, helping learners understand where they need to improve.
4. Risk-Free Environment: Gamification creates a safe space for learners to experiment and learn from their mistakes.

Game vs Learning Activity

The key difference between a game and gamification in

learning lies in the primary objective:

- Game: The primary objective is entertainment, although learning can be a by-product.
- Gamification: The primary objective is learning, with game elements used to enhance that experience.

Effective gamification keeps the learning objectives front and centre, using game elements to reinforce and support those objectives, not overshadow them.

The Perils of Overplaying the Game Element

Gamification can be a double-edged sword. Overemphasis on the gaming aspect can lead to several issues:

1. Distraction from Learning Goals: If the game becomes too engrossing, the core learning objectives may take a backseat.
2. Over-Competitiveness: Intense competition can be demotivating for some learners, especially if the focus shifts from learning to winning.
3. Surface-Level Engagement: Learners might engage with the game superficially without deeply processing the learning material.

Best Practices for Gamification in Learning

1. Balance is Key: Ensure that game elements do not overpower the learning content.
2. Align with Learning Objectives: Every game element should have a clear link to the learning objectives.
3. Inclusive Design: Consider different levels of gaming experience and learning preferences in your design.
4. Feedback Mechanisms: Incorporate constructive feedback to guide learners through their learning journey.

In a nutshell

When done correctly, gamification can be the peak of learning - a summit where engagement, motivation, and enjoyment meet effective knowledge acquisition. It's about harnessing the playful spirit inherent in all of us to make learning not just a task, but an enjoyable and enriching experience. However, like any powerful tool, it must be used judiciously and thoughtfully, always with an eye on the goal: effective and meaningful learning. So, let's roll the dice, play the game, but never lose sight of the learning horizon.

H IS FOR HANDS-ON LEARNING

Imagine sitting in a classroom, absorbing information about swimming. You understand the theory, the movements, the breathing techniques. But it's not until you dive into the water that you truly learn how to swim. It feels like I'm obsessed with swimming – I'm not.

This is the essence of hands-on learning – the powerful process of applying knowledge in a practical, real-world context. In this chapter, we explore the benefits of hands-on learning, particularly its application in the workplace.

The Power of Practical Application

Hands-on learning, or experiential learning, involves actively engaging in an activity to apply and test the knowledge acquired. It's about moving from theory to practice, from abstract to concrete.

It also supports:

1. Enhanced Retention: When you apply what you've learned, you're more likely to retain that information. It's the difference between reading about a concept and doing it.
2. Real-World Skills: Hands-on learning helps develop practical skills that are directly applicable to real-world scenarios, particularly in the workplace.
3. Problem-Solving: Applying learning in a practical environment often involves solving real problems, which enhances critical thinking and decision-making skills.
4. Engagement and Motivation: Learners are generally more engaged and motivated when they can see the practical application of what they're learning.

Applying Learning in the Workplace

1. On-the-Job Training: This is a classic form of hands-on learning. Assign tasks that allow employees to apply new skills in their day-to-day roles.
2. Simulations and Role-Playing: Create simulated environments or role-play scenarios that mimic workplace challenges.
3. Project-Based Learning: Involve learners in projects where they can apply various skills and

knowledge. This also promotes teamwork and collaboration.
4. Mentoring and Shadowing: Pair learners with more experienced colleagues to observe and participate in real-world application of skills.

Overcoming Challenges

While hands-on learning is incredibly beneficial, it comes with its own set of challenges:

1. Resource Intensive: Practical learning can require more resources, time, and planning compared to traditional classroom learning.
2. Risk of Mistakes: Applying skills in a real-world context can lead to mistakes, which, while valuable learning opportunities, may have implications in the workplace. Managers and Leaders need to be well-versed in coaching practices to support colleagues when things go wrong.
3. Varied Learning Pace: Individuals learn at different paces, especially in practical settings. This requires patience and tailored support.

In a nutshell

Hands-on learning is an invaluable component of the learning journey, especially in the workplace. It bridges the gap between theoretical knowledge and practical application, ensuring that learning is not just an intellectual exercise but a tool for real-world effectiveness.

Encouraging and facilitating hands-on learning opportunities within the workplace not only enhances skills but also contributes to a culture of continuous improvement and practical problem-solving. Remember, the true test of knowledge is not in its acquisition, but in its application.

I IS FOR INTEGRATED LEARNING

In a world where change is the only constant, the ability for organisations to learn and adapt swiftly is not just advantageous; it's essential for survival. Integrated learning is about embedding learning seamlessly into the very fabric of everyday work life. This chapter delves into what integrated learning looks like and offers insights for those aiming to weave it effortlessly into their workplace.

The Essence of Integrated Learning

Integrated learning is the harmonious blend of work and learning, where acquiring new skills and knowledge becomes a natural part of the daily workflow. It's not about carving out specific times for learning; instead, it's about learning being as ubiquitous as checking emails or attending meetings.

Characteristics of Integrated Learning

1. Accessibility: Learning resources are easily accessible, be it through digital platforms, in-person workshops, or informal learning groups.
2. Relevance: Learning is closely aligned with the employee's role and career aspirations, and it addresses the immediate needs of the organisation.
3. Flexibility: Learning is not confined to rigid schedules or formats. It adapts to the preferences and schedules of the learner.
4. **Continuous:** Rather than being event-based, learning is ongoing, with opportunities for growth available always.

Implementing Integrated Learning

1. Embed Learning into Daily Tasks: Turn routine tasks into learning opportunities. For example, a regular project debrief could include a learning session on improving processes or incorporating new methodologies.
2. Leverage Technology: Utilise digital platforms like Learning Management Systems (LMS) or mobile apps that allow employees to learn at their own pace and according to their preferences. Let learners seek their learning in a way that suits them best.
3. Encourage Knowledge Sharing: Create a culture where sharing knowledge is valued. This could be

through formal mentorship programs or informal 'coffee and learn' sessions.
4. Personalise Learning Paths: Recognise that one size doesn't fit all. Offer personalised learning paths that cater to the unique career trajectories of each employee.
5. Leadership Involvement: Have leaders model the importance of continuous learning. When senior staff engage in and advocate for learning, it sets a tone for the entire organisation.

Pitfalls to Avoid

1. Information Overload: While making learning resources abundant, avoid overwhelming employees. Offer curated, high-quality content instead.
2. Neglecting Individual Needs: Not all employees learn the same way. Ignoring individual learning styles can lead to disengagement.
3. Lack of Support: Without proper support and recognition, learning initiatives can falter. Ensure there are adequate systems to help employees in their learning journey.

Food for Thought

- How can you make learning an everyday activity in your workplace?
- What technology can you leverage to make learning more accessible and engaging?

- How can you personalise learning to make it more relevant and effective for each employee?
- What strategies can you employ to foster a culture that values and encourages knowledge sharing?

In Conclusion

Integrated learning is the future of workplace development. It's a strategy that recognises the value of continuous, flexible, and accessible learning. By embedding learning into the very heart of an organisation's daily operations, not only do we enhance the skills of our workforce, but we also foster a culture of continuous improvement and adaptability. In today's fast-paced world, this is no longer a luxury; it's a necessity.

J IS FOR 'JUST IN TIME'

In a world where change is the only constant, 'just in time' learning isn't just a buzzword; it's a crucial strategy. It's about delivering the right learning, at the right time, to support the evolving needs of an organisation. Think of it as the Swiss Army Knife of the learning world – compact, versatile, and exactly what you need in a pinch.

Aligning with Company Goals and Objectives

Just in time learning isn't about throwing random bits of training at employees and hoping something sticks. It's about aligning learning with the heartbeat of the company – its goals and objectives. When a company undergoes change, whether it's a shift in strategy, a new product launch, or a restructuring, learning needs to adapt to support these changes, not lag behind them.

Learning as Part of a Communication Strategy

During times of change, communication is king. But we're not just talking about emails and company announcements. Learning can and should be a key part of this communication strategy. It's a way to not only inform but also equip employees with the skills and understanding they need to navigate and embrace change.

Checklist for Delivering 'Just in Time' Learning

1. Understand the Change: What's changing and why? Understanding the nature of the change helps tailor the learning to be relevant and effective.
2. Identify Learning Needs: What do employees need to know or do differently? This could range from new software skills to understanding new company policies.
3. Timing is Everything: Deliver the learning close to when it will be applied. Too early, and people forget; too late, and the opportunity is missed.
4. Flexible Delivery Methods: Use a mix of eLearning, workshops, and microlearning. Different topics and learner preferences may call for different approaches.
5. Communication is Key: Clearly communicate why this learning is important. Help employees see the connection between the learning and the change.

6. Feedback Loops: After the learning, gather feedback. What worked? What didn't? Use this to improve future 'just in time' learning initiatives.
7. Continuous Evaluation: Assess the impact of the learning on performance and adapt as necessary. The goal is to keep the learning agile and responsive.

In Conclusion

'Just in time' learning isn't just about being efficient; it's about being strategic. It's about ensuring that learning is a seamless, integral part of a company's evolution. By following the checklist and keeping learning aligned with company goals and change processes, organisations can ensure they're not just surviving changes, but thriving through them.

As you reflect on this, consider how 'just in time' learning can be integrated into your own organisation. How can you make learning timely, relevant, and a natural part of the company's growth and adaptation journey? Remember, in the fast-paced world of business, sometimes the best learning is the learning that happens just in time.

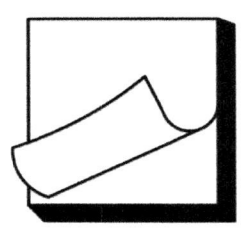

K IS FOR KNOWLEDGE TRANSFER

Imagine if every bit of learning was like a sticky note that firmly sticks to your brain, ready to be used when needed. That's the essence of 'sticky' learning – learning that lasts, is memorable, and easily transferable to real-world applications. In this chapter, we'll explore how to design learning for maximum stickiness and tackle the barriers that often hinder knowledge transfer.

Designing for Stickiness

1. Active Learning: Engage learners actively. This can be through discussions, problem-solving tasks, or hands-on activities. Active participation helps cement learning more effectively than passive listening.
2. Relevance and Context: People retain information better when they see its relevance to their work or

life. Contextualise learning with real-life examples, scenarios, and case studies.
3. Repetition and Spacing: Repetition is the mother of learning. Reinforce key points through spaced repetition – revisiting them over time to deepen understanding and retention.
4. Multisensory Learning: People have different learning styles. Incorporate visual, auditory, and kinaesthetic elements to cater to varied preferences.
5. Emotional Connection: Emotionally engaging content is more likely to be remembered. Use storytelling, relatable characters, or real-life implications to create an emotional bond with the material.

Barriers to Knowledge Transfer

1. Lack of Practice: Without the opportunity to apply new knowledge, learning can fade away. Practical application is crucial.
2. Overload: Cramming too much information into a short time can overwhelm learners, leading to poor retention.
3. Lack of Reinforcement: If new knowledge is not reinforced after the initial learning, it can be quickly forgotten.
4. Irrelevance: Learning that doesn't align with the learner's needs or interests is less likely to stick.

Key Research and Statistics

Several studies highlight the importance of effective knowledge transfer and retention:

- The Forgetting Curve: Research by Ebbinghaus shows that without reinforcement, people forget approximately 50% of new information within an hour and an alarming 70% within 24 hours [1].
- Learning Retention Rates: The National Training Laboratories found that retention rates for lecture-style learning were only 5%, compared to 75% for practical application [2].
- Impact of Active Learning: A study by Freeman et al. (2014) indicated that students in classes with traditional lecturing were 1.5 times more likely to fail than those in classes with active learning [3].

These findings underscore the need for learning experiences that are engaging, interactive, and directly applicable to real-life situations.

In Conclusion

Designing learning for maximum stickiness is not just about delivering content; it's about creating an experience that embeds knowledge deeply into the learner's psyche. As learning professionals, our goal is to ensure that when learners walk away, they carry with them knowledge that sticks, grows, and translates effectively into their everyday work.

L IS FOR LIFELONG LEARNING

In an ever-evolving world, the ability to continuously learn and adapt is not just a skill; it's a superpower. Lifelong learning extends far beyond the conventional classroom setting – it permeates every aspect of our lives. This chapter explores how organisations can cultivate a culture where learning is an ongoing journey, not a destination, and how they can tap into diverse learning channels to nurture this ethos.

Creating a Culture of Lifelong Learning

The cornerstone of lifelong learning is a culture that not only encourages but celebrates continuous personal and professional development. This culture is characterised by curiosity, openness to new ideas, and a proactive approach to learning.

1. Encourage Curiosity and Inquiry: Foster an environment where asking questions and seeking new knowledge is valued. Encourage employees to be inquisitive about their work, the industry, and even broader world affairs.
2. Leadership as Role Models: Leaders should exemplify lifelong learning. Their commitment to their own development can inspire others to follow suit.
3. Recognition and Reward: Acknowledge and reward efforts to learn and grow. This could be through formal recognition programs or informal praise.
4. Create Learning Communities: Encourage the formation of learning groups or communities of practice where employees can share knowledge and learn from each other.

Harnessing Diverse Learning Channels

1. On-the-Job Learning: Much learning happens in the flow of work. Encourage employees to view everyday challenges as learning opportunities.
2. Mentorship Programs: Pairing less experienced employees with mentors can facilitate knowledge transfer and personal growth.
3. Online Courses and Webinars: Leverage the wealth of online learning resources. Encourage staff to engage in online courses, webinars, and virtual workshops relevant to their roles and interests.

4. Conferences and Seminars: Attending industry conferences and seminars can provide insights into current trends and best practices.
5. Social Media and Blogs: Platforms like LinkedIn, industry-specific forums, and educational blogs are valuable sources for the latest thinking and discussions.
6. Book Clubs and Discussion Groups: Foster a love of reading by starting book clubs or discussion groups focused on professional development topics.
7. Cross-Departmental Training: Offer opportunities for employees to learn about different aspects of the business, enhancing their understanding of the organisation.

Encouraging Learning as a Habit

1. Set Personal Learning Goals: Encourage employees to set and pursue their own learning goals, aligned with their career aspirations and personal interests.
2. Time for Learning: Allocate dedicated time for learning activities. This could be a set number of hours per month for employees to engage in learning of their choice.
3. Learning Resources: Provide easy access to learning materials, such as an internal library of books, subscriptions to online courses, or a database of educational materials.
4. Regular Check-Ins: Incorporate discussions about learning and development into regular one-on-ones or performance reviews.

In a nutshell

Lifelong learning is about embracing the idea that our capacity to learn and grow doesn't stop at a certain age or career stage; it continues throughout our lives.

Organisations that harness this power not only create a more skilled and adaptable workforce but also cultivate an environment that is vibrant, dynamic, and ever evolving.

By embedding learning into the DNA of your organisation, you're not just investing in skills – you're nurturing a mindset that can lead to innovation, resilience, and sustained success.

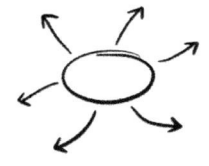

M IS FOR MIND MAPPING

Picture this: you're in a room full of learners, notes in hand, ready to deliver a training session. Now, imagine doing the same without a single note, just a mind map you created. Impressive, right? This chapter is your gateway into the world of mind mapping – a tool that not only supports cognitive function but also empowers you to be a seemingly 'notes-free' facilitator.

What is Mind Mapping?

A mind map is a visual representation of ideas and concepts, originating from a central theme and branching out into related topics. It's like the tree of knowledge, where each branch is a thought, or an idea connected to the main trunk. This tool is not just about jotting down notes; it's about organising thoughts in a way that mirrors how our brain works.

Why Mind Mapping?

1. Enhances Memory and Recall: The brain loves visuals. A mind map, with its branches and colours, is far more memorable than linear notes.
2. Boosts Creativity: It encourages you to think outside the box, making connections you might not have seen before.
3. Improves Understanding: By mapping out ideas, you can see the bigger picture and how concepts interlink.
4. Notes-Free Facilitation: A well-constructed mind map can be a cue for your entire session, reducing your reliance on detailed notes.

Creating a Mind Map: A Step-by-Step Guide

1. Start with the Central Idea: This is the core of your mind map – the 'trunk' of your tree. Write down the main topic or idea you're exploring.
2. Add Main Branches: From the central idea, draw branches for the key subtopics or themes. These are your primary branches – think of them as the main chapters of your topic.
3. Expand with Smaller Branches: For each main branch, add smaller branches to represent specific points or ideas related to that subtopic.
4. Use Keywords and Images: Mind maps work best with keywords, symbols, or images, rather than long sentences. This makes the information more digestible and easier to recall.
5. Colour Coding: Use different colours for different branches or themes. This not only makes your mind map visually appealing but also helps in separating and categorising information.

Different Types of Mind Maps

- Spider Map: Central idea in the middle with main themes branching out like spider legs.
- Flowchart: More structured, showing a sequence of steps or processes.
- Organisational Chart: Hierarchical, perfect for mapping out organisational structures or decision-making processes.

The Power of Appearing Notes-Free

As a facilitator, using a mind map gives you an edge. It creates an impression of mastery over the subject. You appear more engaged with the audience, as you're not constantly referring to your notes. This can make your session more interactive and dynamic. Your audience will trust you more quickly.

In a nutshell

Mind mapping is more than a note-taking technique; it's a cognitive tool that can enhance the way you organise, recall, and present information. So next time you're preparing for a training session, give mind mapping a go. Not only will it help streamline your thoughts, but it will also impress your learners with your seemingly effortless grasp of the material.

And as you master this skill, think about how you can apply mind mapping in other areas – be it planning a project, hacking ideas, or even organising your week. The possibilities are as limitless as your mind's capacity to map them out.

N IS FOR NOW! GET TO THE POINT

In a world where attention spans rival those of goldfish and time is as precious as diamonds, mastering the art of swiftly reaching the 'gold nugget' of learning is not just valuable; it's essential.

This chapter champions a learning approach that quickly delivers the key information and then dedicates time to exploring and applying that concept.

Let's explore why speed learning aligns with the needs of modern learners and organisations, and how to sidestep common pitfalls in designing such learning experiences.

The Rationale for Speed Learning

1. Backing from Research: Studies in cognitive psychology suggest that human attention spans are limited. Research from the University of California points out that focused attention spans may last around 10 to 20 minutes during a lecture [1]. Speed learning taps into this by delivering key points in short, attention-friendly segments.
2. Meeting Learner Needs: Today's learners often juggle multiple responsibilities. Quick, focused learning respects their time constraints and caters to their need for efficiency.
3. Benefits for Organisations: In a business context, time directly correlates with productivity and cost. Speed learning means less time away from work and quicker application of new skills or knowledge.

Implementing Speed Learning

1. Identify the Core Message: What is the essential learning point? Begin with this and eliminate any unnecessary information.
2. Active Learning Techniques: Engage learners immediately with activities, discussions, or problem-solving tasks related to the key concept.
3. Visual Aids and Summaries: Employ infographics, charts, or bullet-point summaries to convey information succinctly.
4. Immediate Application: Provide opportunities for learners to apply what they've learned

straightaway, reinforcing the quick delivery of content.

Pitfalls to Avoid

1. Oversimplification: While brevity is key, simplifying complex topics too much can lead to misunderstandings. Striking a balance is crucial.
2. Lack of Depth: Speed should not sacrifice depth. Ensure that while the delivery is brisk, it still comprehensively covers the necessary breadth of the topic.
3. Neglecting Engagement: Rapid learning can become a monologue if not thoughtfully designed. Keep it interactive to maintain engagement.
4. Information Overload: To be quick, cramming too much information into a short period can overwhelm. Focus on one or two key points per session.

Mastering Speed Learning Design

Designing effective speed learning requires:

1. Clarity in Objectives: Be explicit about what the learner needs to know or do by the end of the session.
2. Focused Content Development: Every piece of content should directly serve the learning objective.

3. Feedback and Adaptation: Regularly seek feedback and be willing to adapt your approach based on what is most effective for your audience.

In a nutshell

The art of getting to the point quickly in learning responds to the modern world's demand for speed and efficiency. By focusing on delivering key concepts swiftly and allowing ample time for exploration and application, learners and organisations can enjoy the benefits of effective and time-efficient learning. Remember, in the race against time, the ability to learn quickly is not just a skill; it's a superpower.

Let's back it up with some Source References:

1. Bradbury, N. A. (2016). Attention span during lectures: 8 seconds, 10 minutes, or more? *Advances in Physiology Education*, 40(4), 509-513. DOI: 10.1152/advan.00109.2016

O IS FOR OBJECTIVE DRIVEN

In the grand tapestry of learning, objectives are the threads that guide us through the labyrinth of information and skills. Without them, we risk wandering aimlessly in the maze of knowledge. Let's explore the significance of setting learning objectives, aligning them with business goals, and ensuring they are met – and, importantly, understanding the consequences when they're not.

Setting Learning Objectives

Think of learning objectives as your GPS system. They help you navigate the learning journey, ensuring you're heading in the right direction. But how do we set these objectives?

1. **Be Specific**: Objectives should be as clear as a bell on a quiet night. Instead of "understand customer service," aim for "identify and apply five key principles of customer service excellence."

2. **Make Them Measurable**: How will you know if the objective has been achieved? "Improve sales skills" is nebulous. "Increase sales conversion rates by 10%" is measurable.
3. **Ensure Relevance**: Objectives should be relevant to the learner's role and future development. Irrelevant objectives are about as useful as a chocolate teapot.
4. **Time-Bound**: Set a realistic timeframe for achieving the objectives. This helps maintain focus and momentum.

Aligning with Business Goals, Vision, and Values

Just as a compass aligns with magnetic north, learning objectives should align with the organisation's goals, vision, and values. This alignment ensures that learning directly contributes to the business's overall direction and success. It's about making sure that the learning journey is not just a solitary hike but a strategic expedition towards the organisation's summit.

Identifying When Objectives Have Been Met

Measuring the attainment of objectives is crucial. It's the difference between thinking you've reached your destination and knowing you have. Methods include assessments, practical demonstrations, feedback from peers and managers, and measuring performance indicators. It's like having checkpoints along the route to confirm you're on the right path.

The Damage of Missing Objectives

Failing to meet learning objectives can be as damaging as a wrong turn on a mountain trail. It can lead to wasted resources, disengaged employees, and a workforce ill-equipped to meet the challenges of their roles. In the worst-case scenario, it can directly impact business performance and competitive edge.

A Sense Check Guide for Setting Objectives

1. Are they aligned with business goals?
2. Are they specific and clear?
3. Can you measure their success?
4. Are they relevant to the learners?
5. Have you set a realistic timeframe?
6. Do they challenge and stretch the learners?

In a nutshell

Objective-driven learning is not just about ticking boxes. It's about embarking on a journey with a clear map and a purpose. It's ensuring that every learning activity moves the individual and the organisation closer to their goals. So, as you set out to chart your learning objectives, remember their power and their purpose. Well-crafted objectives are the compass that guides the learning journey, ensuring it is purposeful, impactful, and aligned with the broader goals of the organisation.

P IS FOR PLAY

When you hear the word 'play', what springs to mind? Children chasing each other in a park, a raucous game of Monopoly, or maybe a nail-biting football match? Well, it's time to broaden that horizon. Play isn't just for children or sports fields; it's a critical component in the world of learning. And no, this isn't about turning every training session into a free-for-all. It's about harnessing the power of play to create more effective, engaging, and memorable learning experiences.

Understanding Play in Learning

Play in learning doesn't mean replacing your PowerPoint slides with hopscotch (though that could be fun). It's about introducing elements of creativity, experimentation, and fun into the learning process.

It's the antithesis of rote learning, where memorisation rules the roost. Playful learning is active, dynamic, and, most importantly, enjoyable.

Lego Serious Play: A Case Study

A quintessential example of play in learning is the 'Lego Serious Play' methodology. Yes, we're talking about those little plastic bricks that have a habit of finding your bare feet in the dark. But in this context, they're tools for problem-solving, idea generation, and team building.

Lego Serious Play involves participants using Lego bricks to build models that represent their thoughts, ideas, and reflections on a given topic. It's not about artistic prowess; it's about visualising complex ideas in a tangible way. This approach fosters open communication, creativity, and a different way of thinking. It's a perfect example of how play can be harnessed to tackle serious business topics in an engaging and effective way.

Why Play Matters

1. Engagement: Let's face it, we could all do with a bit more fun in our lives. Playful learning boosts

engagement, keeping learners interested and involved.
2. Creativity and Innovation: Play encourages out-of-the-box thinking. It's about exploring possibilities without the fear of 'getting it wrong'.
3. Emotional Connection: Playful experiences often stick in our memories more vividly. This emotional connection can enhance learning retention.
4. Stress Reduction: Play can reduce anxiety and stress, creating a more conducive environment for learning.

Bringing Playfulness into Learning Environments

1. Gamification: Introduce game-like elements such as points, levels, and rewards into the learning process. It's about turning learning into a game, not just playing a game.
2. Scenario based: This method allows learners to step into different scenarios and explore various outcomes. It's play with a purpose.
3. Idea Hacking with Props: Use objects like Lego bricks, playdough, or even simple drawing tools to stimulate creative thinking during brainstorming sessions.
4. Interactive Technology: Utilise technology like virtual or augmented reality for immersive, playful learning experiences.
5. Storytelling: Everyone loves a good story. Weave learning content into narratives that are relatable and engaging.

In a nutshell

Play in learning is not about frivolity: it's a serious business. It's about breaking down barriers, encouraging creative thinking, and making the learning process something to look forward to. So, next time you're planning a training session or a learning module, ask yourself: how can I add an element of play to this? How can I make this not just informative, but also enjoyable

> "We don't stop playing because we grow old; we grow old because we stop playing."
> – George Bernard Shaw

Q IS FOR QUESTIONING

Questioning is a fine art in the world of facilitation, akin to an archaeologist gently brushing away layers of soil to reveal hidden treasures. It's not just about asking questions; it's about asking the right questions in the right way. A well-placed question can open doors to deeper understanding, encourage critical thinking, and guide learners to new insights. Let's delve into the types of questions facilitators can use and how to navigate trickier conversational terrains.

Types of Questions and Their Uses

1. Open-Ended Questions: These are the bread and butter of facilitation. They encourage elaboration and discussion. For example, "What are your thoughts on this approach?" or "How do you think this concept applies in your work?"

2. Closed Questions: These are more about garnering specific information and are usually answered with a 'yes' or 'no'. For instance, "Have you used this software before?"
3. Probing Questions: When you need more depth, probing questions are your go-to. They dig deeper. "Can you explain further?" or "What specifically led you to this conclusion?"
4. Reflective Questions: These encourage learners to reflect and self-assess. For example, "How do you feel your approach to this task has evolved?"
5. Hypothetical Questions: Great for stimulating imagination and considering different scenarios. "What would you do if you were faced with X situation?"
6. Leading Questions: These suggest a particular answer and are useful for guiding discussions in a specific direction. "Don't you think that approach might be more effective?"

Managing Difficult Situations with Questions

In challenging situations, questions can be a facilitator's best ally:

1. Defusing Tension: When discussions get heated, use calming questions to bring back focus. "Can we explore why this topic might be causing strong opinions?"
2. Encouraging Participation: To draw in quieter participants, use inviting questions. "I'd love to hear your perspective on this, X."

3. Clarifying and Summarising: If the conversation is going off-track, use questions to refocus. "Can we summarise the key points we've agreed on so far?"
4. Dealing with Resistance: When you encounter resistance, try to understand the root cause. "Can you help me understand your concerns about this approach?"

In a nutshell

As a facilitator, your questions are more than enquiries; they're tools for guiding, clarifying, and exploring. They help create a dynamic learning environment where ideas can be shared openly and explored thoroughly. Remember, the art of questioning is not just about what you ask, but how and when you ask it.

The next time you find yourself in a facilitation role, consider not only the content of your questions but also their impact and timing. Your questions have the power to unlock potential, inspire thought, and lead to meaningful insights, so wield them with both care and confidence.

R IS FOR ROLE PLAY (UNFORTUNATELY)

There's a phrase that strikes fear into the hearts of many a learner: "Let's do a role play." Cue the nervous shuffling of feet, the averted gazes, the sudden, intense interest in the fine print on the handout. Role play, for all its theoretical merits, often feels like being asked to perform a Shakespearean monologue in front of Simon Cowell. It's time to rethink this age-old practice in the learning environment – for me it's always an indicator of an out of touch facilitator.

The Theory vs Reality of Role Play

Theoretically, role play is a solid learning tool. It's supposed to help people practice real-life situations in a safe, controlled environment. But let's face it, for many, the experience is far from educational. It's about as comfortable as a hedgehog in a balloon factory. The focus inadvertently shifts from learning to acting, leaving participants more worried about their thespian skills (or lack thereof) than the actual learning objectives. Think back to those biases...

The Learner's Experience

Imagine being asked to role play a difficult conversation with a manager or a sensitive negotiation. For many, this is the stuff of nightmares. It's not just the fear of performing in front of others; it's the anxiety of being judged, the worry of looking foolish, and the pressure to 'act'. The result? A room full of stressed learners, where the learning takes a backseat to performance anxiety.

Practical Alternatives to Role Play

1. Guided Scenarios: Instead of full-blown role plays, use guided scenarios where learners discuss and analyse a situation collectively. This takes the spotlight off individuals and allows for a more inclusive discussion.
2. Case Studies: Dive into real-life case studies and explore them in detail. Encourage learners to discuss what they would do differently, offering a more analytical approach to learning.
3. Interactive Storytelling: Create a story around a scenario and have learners contribute to how the story unfolds. This can be done in groups and is less intimidating than traditional role play.

4. Video Analysis: Show videos of scenarios and have participants analyse and discuss them. This can provide clear examples of what to do (or not to do) without putting someone on the spot.
5. Skill Practice in Pairs: If you must have an interactive element, keep it low-key. Pair up learners to practice specific skills or have discussions, rather than full-on role plays.

Remember, It's About the Learner

As learning professionals, it's crucial to remember that what works for one person may terrify another. The goal of any learning activity should be to enhance understanding and skills, not to showcase dramatic flair.

In a nutshell

It's time to let go of traditional role play and embrace alternatives that keep the focus firmly on learning, not acting. By doing so, we create a more comfortable and effective learning environment. So, next time you're tempted to say, "Let's role play," maybe, just maybe, don't. Remember, the best learning happens when participants feel safe, comfortable, and focused on the task at hand, not on their impending Oscar nomination.

S IS FOR STORYTELLING

Once upon a time, in a world brimming with data and information, there was a powerful tool called storytelling. This isn't just about fairy tales or campfire yarns. It's about the profound impact that a well-told story can have in the realm of learning. Let's embark on a journey to uncover why storytelling is a facilitators secret weapon and how to wield it effectively.

The Magic of Storytelling

Storytelling is as old as humanity itself, a fundamental way in which we communicate, connect, and convey information. In learning, stories are more than entertainment; they're vessels that carry complex ideas in a relatable package. A good story can illuminate concepts, evoke emotions, and, most importantly, stick in our memories long after facts and figures fade.

The Emotive Hook

A story, unlike a list of bullet points, has an emotive hook – it engages not just the mind but the heart. Think about the last time a story moved you, made you laugh, or brought a tear to your eye. That emotional connection is a powerful glue for memory. When learners connect emotionally with the content, they're more likely to absorb and remember it.

Constructing a Story for Learning

1. Start with the 'Why': Why is this story relevant? Start from the perspective of its importance to your learners.
2. Create Relatable Characters: Learners should see themselves in the story. The characters' challenges and triumphs should mirror their own.
3. Build a Narrative Arc: A story should have a beginning, middle, and end – set the scene, introduce the conflict or challenge, and then resolve it.
4. Use Descriptive Language: Engage the senses with vivid language to bring the story to life.
5. Include a Moral or Lesson: Every good learning story should have a clear takeaway or lesson.

The Story Must Be Yours to Tell

Authenticity in storytelling is crucial. It's important to tell stories that you have a right to tell – ones that come from your experiences, or that you're authorised to share. This isn't just about avoiding plagiarism; it's about the integrity and genuineness that resonate with listeners.

When Not to Tell a Story

Storytelling is powerful, but it's not always the right tool. Avoid storytelling when:

1. The Detail is Crucial: If the specifics and nuances of information are vital, a straightforward presentation might be more appropriate.
2. The Story Overwhelms the Message: If the story overshadows the learning objective, it's counterproductive.
3. Sensitivity and Respect: In topics that require a high degree of sensitivity or are deeply personal, tread carefully with storytelling.

The Power of Stories in Action

Consider the impact of stories in learning environments like TED Talks, where complex ideas are often woven into personal narratives. Or think about case studies in business schools, where real-world business dilemmas are presented as stories for students to unravel.

In a nutshell

Incorporating storytelling into your learning strategy isn't just about spinning a good yarn; it's about engaging your learners on a deeper level. A well-crafted story can turn a forgettable lesson into an unforgettable learning experience. So, next time you're preparing a lesson or a presentation, think about how you can turn your information into a story that will resonate, engage, and, most importantly, be remembered. After all, the stories we tell can transform the way we learn, teach, and understand the world around us.

T IS FOR TIMETASTIC

It feels like we've been here before. It's so important, I'm talking about it again.

Have you ever been stuck in a meeting that was meant to last 30 minutes but stretched into two hours?

Remember that feeling of frustration, thinking, "Why couldn't they just get to the point?" Now, consider this in the context of learning. We've all sat through lengthy lectures or courses, and by the end, often find ourselves struggling to retain the main message.

There's a myth out there that says for learning to be effective, it must be long-winded. But what if we could do away with this misconception and understand that sometimes, shorter is sweeter?

Less Time, More Value

Our brains are hardwired to grasp the crux of a matter quickly. Think about it. A catchy song doesn't need 20 minutes to stick in your head. A meme doesn't need a five-page essay to convey its humour. So why should important learning points require hours?

Consider the ancient proverb: *"Brevity is the soul of wit."* Short, crisp, and loaded with wisdom. That's what we need in learning, skilfully distilled to the 'golden nugget' of learning.

The Beauty of Focus

When you have only a short time to convey a message, it demands clarity. There's no room for fluff or unnecessary jargon. It's about understanding the key message and delivering it in the most impactful way possible. By reducing the learning time, we're not compromising on quality. Instead, we're maximising the punch each minute packs.

Practice Makes Perfect, Not Prolonged Lectures

Imagine you're learning to ride a bike. Would you rather spend hours hearing about the history of bicycles, the various parts, and the physics of balance, or would you prefer a quick rundown followed by getting on the bike and trying it out?

Learning, especially in a real-world environment, thrives on practice and experience. When we spend less time on long lectures and more time on active exploration, the learning not only sticks better but also becomes more enjoyable.

Setting the Stage for Application

By cutting down the lecture time, we're also allowing learners more time to apply their newfound knowledge. This means they can immediately reinforce what they've learned, making it more likely to stay with them in the long run.

Imagine learning a quick tip on communication. Instead of a three-hour seminar, you get a 10-minute burst of valuable insight. You can then spend the rest of your day consciously applying this tip in your conversations, solidifying the learning through real-world practice.

Challenge for You

The next time you're about to teach or share something, whether it's a corporate training or a fun fact with a friend, pause for a moment. Ask yourself: "How can I make this message crisp, clear, and quick?" Trim the excess, focus on the core, and then let the learning bloom in practice.

In a nutshell

We live in a fast-paced world. Time is precious. Let's respect our learners by offering them powerful insights without holding them hostage to long-drawn-out sessions.

Let's be timetastic and get to the point. Quickly.

U IS FOR UNLEARNING

You know that old chestnut, "You can't teach an old dog new tricks"? Well, I'd like to challenge it. Sometimes, the obstacle isn't learning the new trick; it's about letting go of the old one. That's where unlearning comes in.

What is Unlearning?

Unlearning isn't about forgetting. It's about being open to seeing things from a fresh perspective, shedding preconceived notions, and making room for new ideas. Just as a painter needs a blank canvas to create a masterpiece, sometimes we need to clear out old, entrenched habits and beliefs to make way for innovation.

Why is it So Tricky?

1. **Comfort Zone**: We've always done it like that, haven't we? It's comfortable and familiar. But just because something feels comfortable doesn't mean it's still right or effective.
2. **Fear of the Unknown**: Treading unfamiliar territory can be daunting. We worry about making mistakes or appearing foolish. But remember, every expert was once a beginner.
3. **Ego**: Admitting that a long-held belief or practice might be outdated can feel like a blow to one's pride. But growth often requires a bit of humility.

Steps to Encourage Unlearning

1. **Challenge the Status Quo**: Next time you hear, "We've always done it like this," ask, "Is there a better way?"
2. **Foster Curiosity**: Encourage questions. Being curious naturally leads to challenging old beliefs and exploring new perspectives.
3. **Safe Environment**: Create a space where making mistakes is okay. If people aren't afraid of getting things wrong, they'll be more open to trying something new.
4. **Continuous Feedback**: Regular, constructive feedback helps in refining new skills and approaches, nudging out the old ones.

Practical Ways for Learning Professionals

1. **Use Real-world Examples**: Show how new methods have succeeded in other contexts.

Demonstrating tangible benefits can be convincing.
2. **Collaborative Learning**: Encourage group discussions. Sometimes, just hearing a different viewpoint can jolt someone out of their fixed mindset.
3. **Role-playing**: This technique can help individuals see things from a different perspective, aiding the unlearning process.
4. **Refresher Courses**: Regularly update training materials to ensure they reflect the latest in industry standards and practices.

In a nutshell

Unlearning isn't about disregarding our past experiences or knowledge. It's about understanding that the world, and our place in it, is constantly evolving. And to evolve with it, we sometimes need to take a step back, re-evaluate, and be willing to let go.

So, the next time you find yourself clinging to the phrase, "We've always done it like that," take a deep breath, open your mind, and embrace the exciting world of unlearning. Because sometimes, the path to acquiring new knowledge starts with letting go of the old.

V IS FOR VALUES CENTRED LEARNING

In the tapestry of organisational learning, the threads of company values are integral to the overall design. Values aren't just words on a website or posters on a wall; they are the guiding principles that shape every aspect of a company's culture and operations, including learning. This chapter delves into the significance of integrating values into learning interventions and the ramifications of a misalignment between learning initiatives and organisational values.

Integrating Values in Learning Interventions

Values-centred learning ensures that every educational activity reflects and reinforces what the company stands for. It's about making values tangible through learning experiences.

1. Reflecting Values in Learning Content: Develop training materials that exemplify core values. For instance, if 'innovation' is a key value, include case studies of innovative practices within the organisation.
2. Values in Action: Use real-life scenarios and role-plays that require learners to apply company values in decision-making processes.
3. Leadership Involvement: Encourage leaders to participate in training sessions, not just as facilitators, but as active proponents of the organisation's values.
4. Rewarding Value-Aligned Behaviours: In learning and development programmes, include recognition for learners who exemplify company values in their approach.

Aligning Learning with Organisational Goals

Learning interventions should not only impart skills but also align with the strategic direction of the company. When learners understand how their development contributes to broader organisational goals, learning becomes more meaningful and impactful.

1. Goal-Oriented Learning: Design learning objectives that directly support organisational goals.
2. Communicating the 'Why': Clearly articulate how each learning intervention aligns with both

company values and goals. This enhances engagement and buy-in from learners.
3. Feedback and Evaluation: Regularly gather feedback to ensure learning interventions remain aligned with organisational values and goals.

Consequences of Misalignment

When learning interventions don't align with organisational values, several issues can arise:

1. Reduced Engagement: Employees may feel less engaged if they sense a disconnect between what they're learning and the values they're expected to uphold.
2. Conflicting Messages: Mixed messages can lead to confusion about what the organisation truly prioritises.
3. Cultural Erosion: Over time, the organisational culture can weaken if employees perceive that values are not genuinely integrated into all aspects of the organisation, including learning.

In a nutshell

Values-centred learning is not just about compliance with company principles; it's about weaving these principles into the very fabric of learning and development. It ensures that learning interventions are not only effective in skill development but also in fostering a strong, values-driven culture. In essence, when learning and values go hand in hand, they create a powerful synergy that drives both individual and organisational success. Remember, in the pursuit of knowledge and skills, it's the underlying values that provide direction and purpose.

W IS FOR WORKPLACE LEARNING

In the bustling arena of workplace learning, there's a popular model that's been both a guiding star and a subject of debate: the 70:20:10 rule. Before we delve into the modern landscape of work-based learning, let's demystify this rule and explore how the concept of learning on the job has evolved.

Demystifying the 70:20:10 Rule

The 70:20:10 model for learning and development suggests that individuals obtain 70% of their knowledge from job-related experiences, 20% from interactions with others, and 10% from formal educational events. Initially proposed in the 1980s based on research by Morgan McCall, Robert Eichinger, and Michael Lombardo at the Center for Creative Leadership, this model was derived from a small sample size and primarily focused on successful managers' experiences.

While the 70:20:10 rule has been influential, it's crucial to note that the world of work and learning has changed dramatically since its conception. The digital revolution, a shift in workforce demographics, and changes in work patterns (like remote working) have transformed how and where we learn.

It's testament to sticky learning – it was simple to explore, it was memorable. The phrase 70:20:10 has stuck. See also.... Unlearning!

The Current State of Work-based Learning

Today's work-based learning is more dynamic and diverse, transcending the boundaries of the 70:20:10 framework. Recent studies and trends indicate a more blended and flexible approach to learning at work:

1. Integration of Digital Learning: With the advent of eLearning platforms, mobile learning apps, and virtual reality (VR) training, digital learning is becoming a significant component of work-based learning.

2. Informal vs Formal Learning: There's a growing recognition of the importance of informal learning opportunities, such as mentoring, shadowing, and on-the-job problem-solving.
3. Customisation and Personalisation: Modern learning approaches are increasingly tailored to individual needs and career paths, moving away from a one-size-fits-all model.
4. Learning Culture and Continuous Development: Organisations are fostering cultures of continuous learning and development, recognising that employee learning is ongoing and multifaceted.

New Findings in Work-based Learning

Recent studies have suggested alternative models and approaches:

- Bersin by Deloitte: Their research highlights the importance of a continuous learning culture, where learning is part of the daily workflow [1].
- Towards Maturity: Their benchmark studies suggest that high-performing learning organisations are more likely to integrate learning into the workflow and support it with technology [2].

In a nutshell

The landscape of work-based learning is vast and varied,

far beyond the confines of the 70:20:10 rule. As learning professionals, it's essential to adapt and evolve with the changing times, embracing new technologies, methodologies, and approaches. Work-based learning today is about creating ecosystems of learning that support continuous development and adapt to the unique needs of each organization and learner.

Let's get sourcey:

1. Bersin, J. (2019). *The Corporate Learning Factbook 2019: Benchmarks, Trends, and Analysis of the U.S. Training Market.* Bersin by Deloitte.
2. Towards Maturity. (2020). *Benchmark Report 2020: Learning in the Flow of Work.* [Online] Available at: https://towardsmaturity.org/2020benchmark/

Remember, the goal is not to adhere rigidly to a model but to create an environment where learning is as natural and integral to work as the work itself.

X IS FOR X FACTOR

Let's face it. X could only mean X Factor in this book. The certain something that sets learning apart from everything else it touches. With the letter X, it was that or Xylophone – and even I can't make that work in the context of learning (although I'll never stop trying).

So let's get on with the story…

Picture this: a learning experience so captivating that it leaves the participants not just educated, but genuinely awestruck. This is the essence of the 'X Factor' in learning - crafting experiences that are not just informative but also profoundly engaging and memorable. Let's explore the art of creating this 'wow' factor in learning, focusing on every facet from design to delivery, and how to truly make learning resonate on a human level.

The Art of Engaging Design

1. Storytelling: Weave learning content into compelling narratives. Stories create emotional connections, making learning more relatable and memorable.
2. Visual Impact: Utilise high-quality visuals and multimedia. An aesthetically pleasing and visually stimulating environment can significantly enhance engagement.
3. Interactivity: Move away from passive learning models. Incorporate elements that require active participation, such as simulations or activities.
4. Customisation: Tailor learning experiences to the audience. Personalisation makes learning more relevant, thus more engaging.

Crafting an Immersive Learning Environment

1. Contextual Relevance: Design scenarios that mirror real-life situations. This relevance helps learners see the direct application of their learning.
2. Sensory Engagement: Engage multiple senses. Use audio-visual aids, hands-on activities, and even smell elements if relevant.
3. Safe Space for Exploration: Create an environment where learners feel comfortable to experiment, make mistakes, and learn from them.
4. Dynamic Spaces: Use physical or virtual learning spaces dynamically. Changing settings throughout

the session can keep energy levels high and maintain interest.

The Role of a Brilliant Facilitator

1. Charisma and Connection: A facilitator should have the ability to connect with the audience, using charisma to engage and maintain interest.
2. Adaptability: Be prepared to adjust techniques based on the audience's response. A great facilitator can read the room and pivot as needed.
3. Passion and Energy: Enthusiasm is contagious. A facilitator's passion for the subject can significantly enhance learner engagement.
4. Empathy and Understanding: Show genuine interest in learners' needs and experiences. This builds trust and encourages more open, honest participation.

Human-Centred Learning: What It Looks and Feels Like

Human-centred learning is about recognising that at the heart of every learning experience is a person – with unique needs, experiences, and emotions. It's:

- Empathetic: Understanding and addressing the real needs and challenges of the learners.

- Engaging: Capturing and maintaining interest through compelling content and delivery.
- Empowering: Enabling learners to apply their knowledge in practical, meaningful ways.

Unleashing Human-Centred Learning in the Workplace

1. Continuous Feedback Loop: Regularly gather and act on feedback to ensure learning remains relevant and engaging.
2. Learner Advocacy: Involve learners in the design process. Their insights can be invaluable in creating truly engaging experiences.
3. Cultural Alignment: Ensure learning experiences align with the organisation's culture. This creates a sense of familiarity and relevance.
4. Technology as an Enabler: Use technology not as a crutch, but as a tool to enhance the human aspects of learning.

In a nutshell

Creating the 'wow' in learning is an art form that requires a deep understanding of human psychology, creativity in design, and excellence in execution. It's about crafting experiences that are not just intellectually stimulating but also emotionally engaging and deeply human. In the world of work, where learning can sometimes feel like a chore, infusing the X Factor can transform it into an experience that is eagerly anticipated and fondly remembered. Remember, at the core of exceptional learning experiences are the people they are designed to inspire and empower.

Y IS FOR YIELD

Investing in learning is a bit like planting a seed. You nurture it, watch it grow, and eventually, it bears fruit. But just as in agriculture, in the world of learning, it can be tough to predict exactly what yield your efforts will produce. How do you measure the return on your investment (ROI) in learning when the fruits of your labour often take time to ripen?

The Challenge of Measuring ROI

It's not as simple as checking a balance sheet. The impact of learning on performance can be as subtle as improved morale or as significant as a spike in sales. So how do you put a number on something like confidence or collaboration?

Simplicity in Measurement

Let's break it down to basics. Think about what you can observe and measure:

1. **Skills Before and After**: It's like a before-and-after photo for competencies. Assess skill levels prior to the learning programme and then again afterward. Improvement? That's a direct yield.
2. **Job Performance Metrics**: If your customer service team went through training, check the satisfaction scores. If your sales team learned new techniques, monitor the sales numbers. Changes in these figures can indicate the effectiveness of the learning programme.
3. **Time to Proficiency**: How long does it take a newcomer to reach a certain level of proficiency before the programme versus after? Faster upskilling means you're getting more bang for your buck.

Quality Over Quantity

Remember, the richest yield isn't always the most abundant. It's not about churning out hundreds of trained employees who forget what they've learned in a week. It's about meaningful, lasting development that contributes to individual and organisational goals.

Cost Versus Value

It's easy to look at the invoice for a training programme and balk at the cost. But take a moment to consider value over cost. Cheap training that yields no change is more expensive than a pricier programme that elevates your team to new heights.

The Reflective ROI

Consider reflective questions to gauge ROI:

- How has the work environment improved post-training?
- Can you see a change in how your team approaches problems?
- Are employees sharing their new knowledge, creating a ripple effect of learning?

These softer metrics are a form of ROI not to be overlooked.

Asking the Right Questions

Towards the end of any learning programme, don't just ask if the participants liked it. Ask how they will apply it. Better yet, check in a month later to see if they're still applying it. What did they learn? What have they forgotten? What was useful? What learning have they chosen to ignore?

In a nutshell

It's about looking beyond the immediate costs and seeing the longer-term value. So what can you take from this? What simple measures will you put in place to assess the yield of your learning programmes? How will you ensure that your investment is not just a cost but a catalyst for growth?

Ask yourself:

- What metrics matter most to my organisation?
- How can I track the progress in these areas before and after learning interventions?
- What qualitative changes should I be observing in the workforce?
- And perhaps most crucially, how will I define 'success' in the context of learning?

In the end, the true yield of your learning investment might just be the progress you can't measure in numbers alone, but in the stories of those who have grown because of it.

Z IS FOR ZEIGARNIK EFFECT

Zeigarnik Effect – now there's a term that doesn't roll off the tongue every day unless you're a psychologist or a fan of impressively obscure words.

But behind this tongue-twister is a concept that's surprisingly relevant and incredibly useful in the world of learning.

What is the Zeigarnik Effect?

Named after the Soviet psychologist Bluma Zeigarnik, who first studied the phenomenon in the 1920s, the Zeigarnik Effect refers to our tendency to remember uncompleted or interrupted tasks better than completed ones. In simple terms, when you start something and don't finish it, your brain keeps it on the front burner.

Why It's Vital for Learning

This quirk of memory can be a powerful tool in learning. When learners are engaged in a task that's interrupted, they're more likely to remember what they were doing. It's like your brain keeps nagging you about that half-finished crossword puzzle.

For learning experts and learners, harnessing this effect can lead to more effective retention and engagement.

Harnessing the Zeigarnik Effect in Learning

1. **Breaking Up Content**: Instead of delivering long, uninterrupted sessions, break up the content. Leave learners with a cliff-hanger or an unresolved problem. This keeps their brains ticking over the topic even after the session.
2. **Interactive Learning Sessions**: Create sessions where learners start a task but don't finish it until the next session. This could be a complex problem, a case study, or a project.
3. **Staggered Information Release**: Release learning materials in stages rather than all at once. This can create a sense of anticipation and keeps learners coming back for more.
4. **Reflection Periods**: Incorporate periods where learners stop to reflect on what they've learned so

far, but don't give them all the answers. Let them stew a bit!

Practical Examples

Imagine a workshop where you start a group activity but stop it midway. Or an online course that ends a module with an unresolved case study. These scenarios leverage the Zeigarnik Effect by leaving learners with a cognitive itch they're eager to scratch.

In a nutshell

So, the next time you're planning a learning activity, throw in a bit of Zeigarnik Effect. It's a bit like a TV series ending on a cliff-hanger – it keeps your learners eagerly anticipating the next episode. And while 'Zeigarnik' might not be a word you use every day, incorporating its principle can make every day learning stickier and engaging.

Remember, effective learning isn't just about what happens during the training session; it's also about what lingers in the mind long after. Use the Zeigarnik Effect to your advantage and watch as it transforms the learning experience from a fleeting moment into a lasting memory.

Time to get sourcey:

- Zeigarnik, B. (1927). On finished and unfinished tasks. In *A Source Book of Gestalt Psychology* (pp. 300-314). Routledge & Kegan Paul.
- McLeod, S. (2018). Zeigarnik effect. Simply Psychology. [Online] Available at: https://www.simplypsychology.org/zeigarnik-effect.html

AND NOW... 1-8

I thought it might be more practical to offer some clear steps to achieve better learning in your organisation. If you do these 8 things, you will transform learning in your workplace.

So here goes...

1. Understand the unique needs, goals, and ambition of your organisation
2. Implement a blend of traditional and modern learning methodologies
3. Encourage a culture of continuous learning and feedback
4. Utilise technology to enhance and personalise the learning experience without replacing the human
5. Foster collaborative learning environments
6. Evaluate and iterate programmes regularly
7. Support and develop facilitators for optimal impact
8. Prioritise hands-on, experiential learning opportunities

It's as simple as that! Clearly, to implement a learning strategy that covers the entire A-8 takes resource, time, expertise, and budget, but I hope this book gives a little insight into what's important to me, when it comes to learning.

It's a topic that I'm never likely to stop talking about. There's probably a few more books inside me about a variety of different learning topics.

I'd love to keep the conversation going with you.

ABOUT THE AUTHOR

Chris Duncan-Scott is co-founder at Acceler8 – the playful learning and development consultancy that inspires workplaces around the world where everyone can #BeHappyBeHuman.

Chris started his career in the hospitality sector, where his curiosity about people was ignited. With plenty of operational experience under his belt, he moved into the learning and development environment and has worked with many of the world's leading brands to supercharge their people engagement efforts.

From retail, skincare, and manufacturing to logistics, aviation, fintech, hospitality and technology – the work Chris has achieved at Acceler8 probably influences your daily life in some way shape or form.

In 'The A-8 of Learning', Chris shares his own learning from those many years' experience, giving you everything you need for a winning learning strategy in your organisation.

Chris lives with his husband David and their dog Bo in Brighton, England. He loves the sea and can often be found enjoying the beach with his family.

www.acceler8.global

Printed in Great Britain
by Amazon